BASKETBALL'S Most CONTROVERSIAL PLAYS

YOU MAKE the CALL!

by Heather E. Schwartz

CAPSTONE PRESS
a capstone imprint

Published by Capstone Press, an imprint of Capstone
1710 Roe Crest Drive, North Mankato, Minnesota 56003
capstonepub.com

Library of Congress Cataloging-in-Publication Data
is available on the Library of Congress website.
ISBN: 9798875257377 (hardcover)
ISBN: 9798875257322 (paperback)
ISBN: 9798875257339 (ebook PDF)

Summary: The officials made their calls. Now it's your turn to take an in-depth look at three controversial basketball plays and make your own call. Do you agree with the officials?

Editorial Credits
Editor: Christianne Jones; Designer: Tracy Davies; Media Researcher: Svetlana Zhurkin; Production Specialist: Whitney Shaefer

Image Credits
Associated Press: Ben Margot, 7, Marcio Jose Sanchez, 24, Michael Wyke, 20, Pamela Smith, 15; Getty Images: © 2024 NBAE/David Sherman, 13, © 2024 NBAE/Logan Riely, 19, AFP/Staff, 6, Bruce Bennett, 29 (left), Carmen Mandato, 18, 21, 22, Elsa, 4, 14, 16, Ethan Miller, 11, Ezra Shaw, 27, John E. Moore III, 8, Lachlan Cunningham, 25, 26, Paras Griffin, 9; Newscom: ZUMApress/Detroit News, 5; Shutterstock: Andrey Burmakin, cover (bottom), Lana Sham, back cover, 17, 23, 28, 29 (right), Muhammad Muhdi (dotted background), cover (top) and throughout, Ron Alvey, 10

Words in **BOLD** are in the glossary.

Printed and bound in China. PO 6459

TABLE OF CONTENTS

DEBATABLE DECISIONS

Fancy footwork. **Precise** passing. Dynamic dribbling. These elements make any basketball game exciting to watch. Throw in a few dramatic slam dunks and long-range shots, and you can't look away. Which team will win?

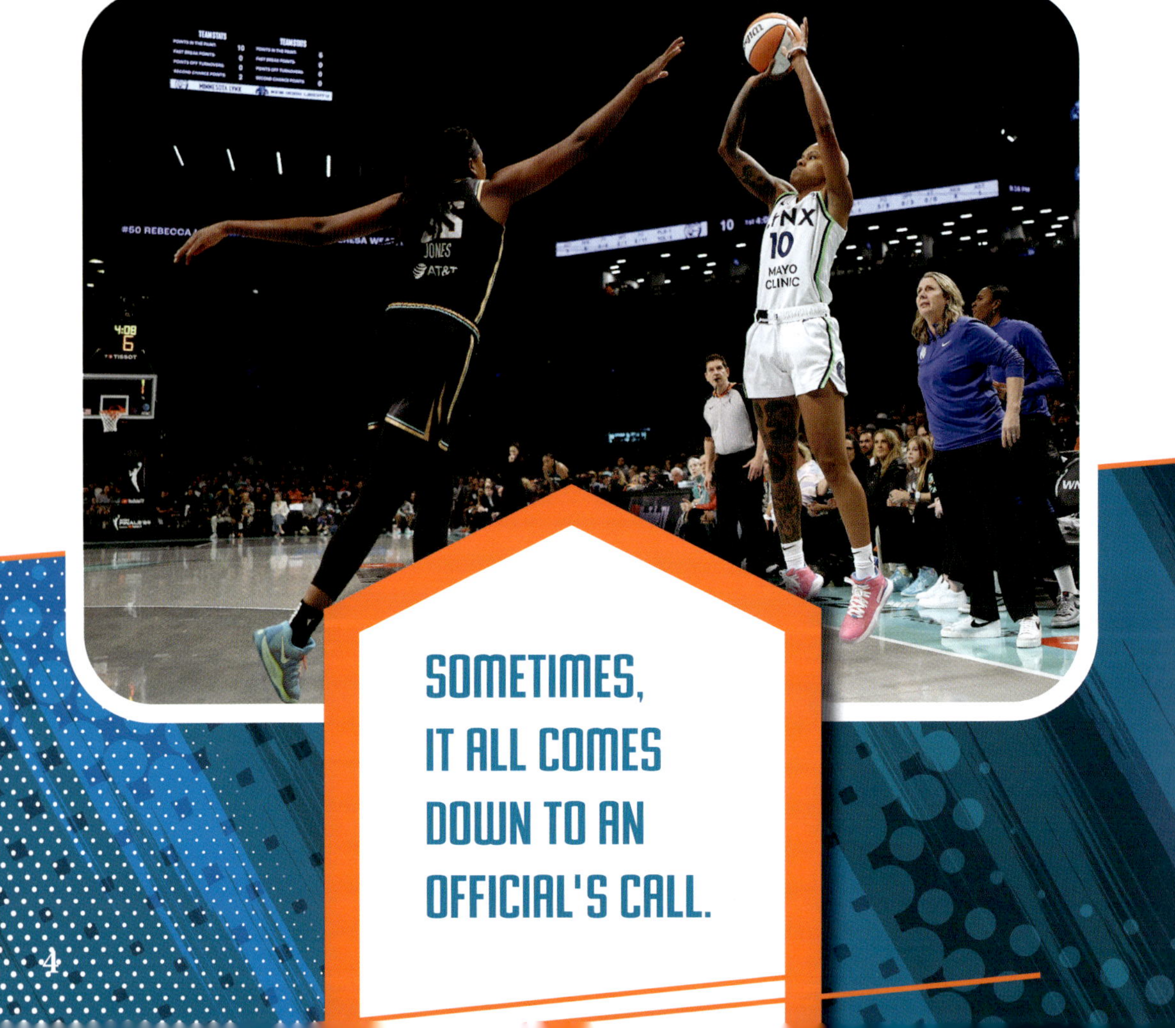

SOMETIMES, IT ALL COMES DOWN TO AN OFFICIAL'S CALL.

Take the 1988 NBA Finals. With 14 seconds left in Game 6, officials called a foul on Detroit Pistons player Bill Laimbeer. The LA Lakers' Kareem Abdul-Jabbar got two free throws.

BUT AFTER THE LAKERS WON, REPLAYS SHOWED LAIMBEER NEVER TOUCHED ABDUL-JABBAR.

Another controversial call came during the 1972 Olympic Games. It happened during the men's basketball final. In the last three seconds, the U.S. was in the lead.

THEN, THE OFFICIALS RESET THE CLOCK, LEADING TO A SOVIET UNION VICTORY.

In both cases, the officials' calls changed the outcome of the game. Were those historic calls the right ones? How would you handle the pressure of being a referee? As you read these stories, put yourself in the ref's shoes.

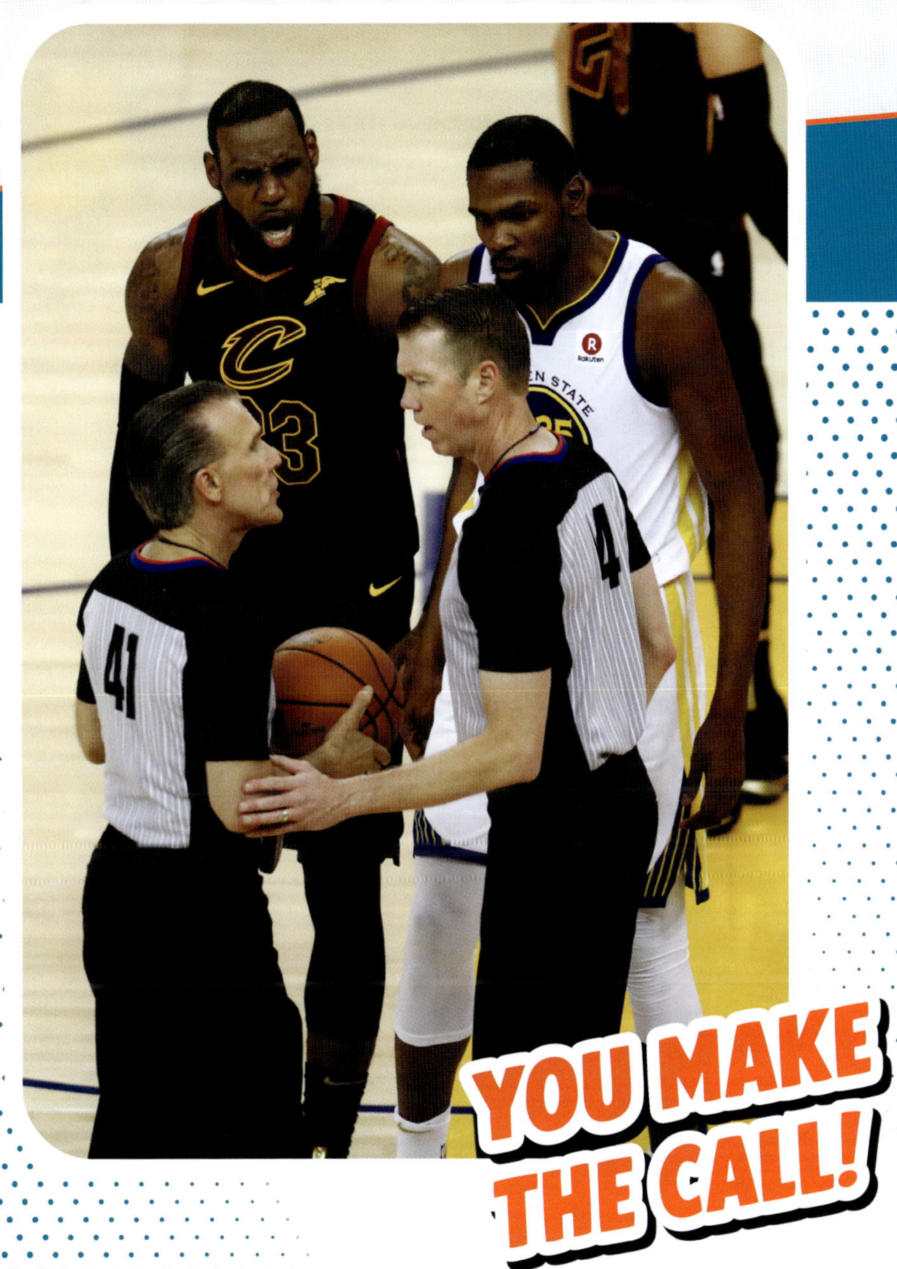

CHAPTER 1

THE IMPORTANCE OF REFEREES

Officials play an important role in basketball. It doesn't matter if the game is between high school teams, college teams, professional teams, or anything in between. It's their job to make sure players play by the rules.

OFFICIALS MAY NOT MAKE THE CALLS PLAYERS WANT.

They may not make the calls the fans want. They have to make quick decisions in a fast-paced game. They make mistakes. But their focus is on fairness and doing the best job they can do.

In basketball, a small team of officials generally includes a head referee plus one or two umpires. Basketball officials go through a lot of training. They learn the rules for each position on the court. They study rule books and manuals. They attend meetings and lectures. They take a written exam.

Most officials start at youth basketball games. They work their way up to officiating college and professional games. In the NBA, officials are well paid.

THEY CAN EARN BETWEEN $150,000 AND $550,000 PER YEAR.

On the job, officials use what they know and what they see to make the calls they believe are correct. They also watch replays on video to view different angles and get a closer look at questionable plays.

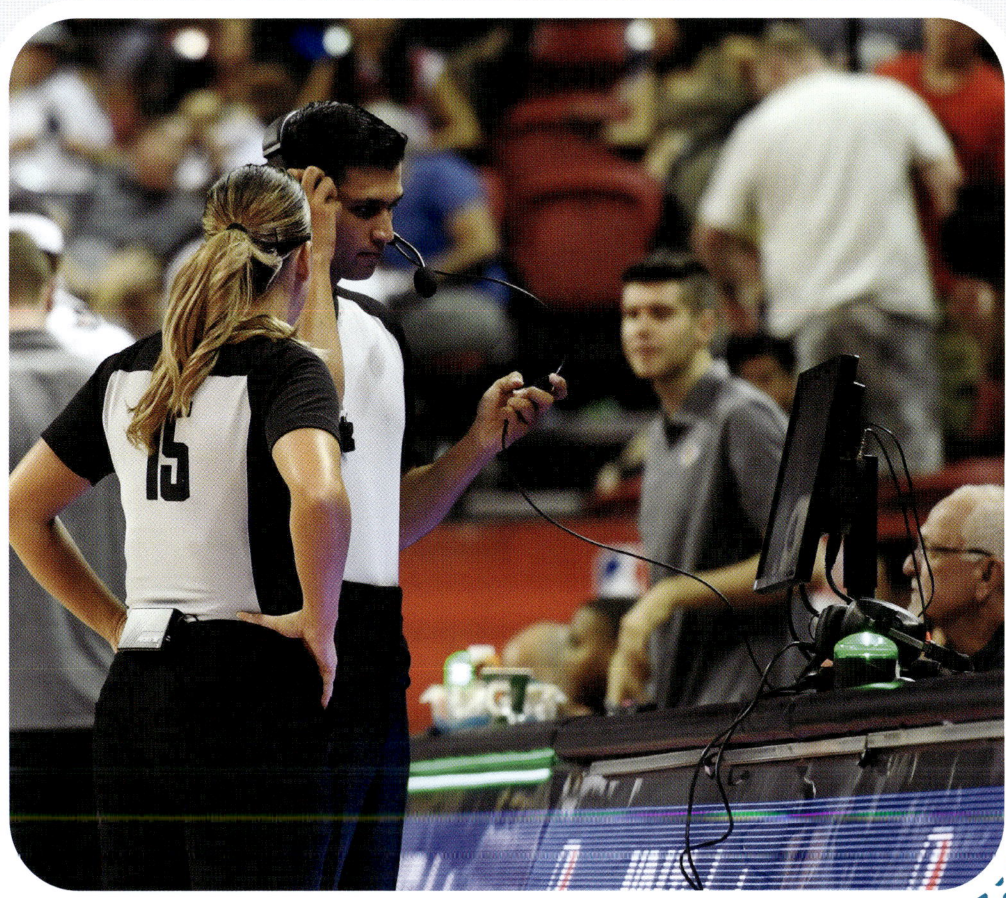

TIME OUT

At the start of the 2014–15 season, the NBA built a Replay Center for quick replay reviews. That season, more than 80 percent of the replays resulted in calls being **upheld**.

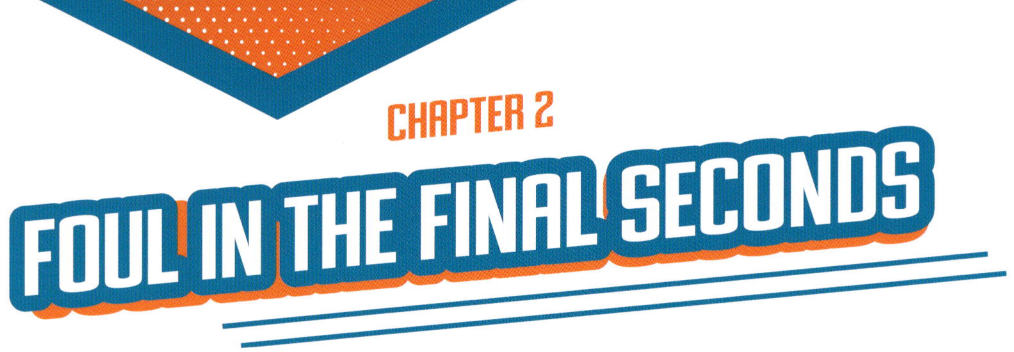

CHAPTER 2

FOUL IN THE FINAL SECONDS

It was a winner-take-all game. With 5.2 seconds left on the clock, the Minnesota Lynx led the New York Liberty 60–58. The dramatic **conclusion** to Game 5 of the 2024 WNBA Finals was **destined** to end in a Lynx victory—or was it?

New York Liberty forward Breanna Stewart caught the inbounds pass near the basket. Minnesota Lynx forward Alanna Smith posted up below the basket to defend her. Smith's arms and body were straight. Stewart jumped up, running into Smith as she shot the ball—and missed!

BUT THAT WASN'T THE END OF THE GAME. OFFICIALS CALLED A CONTACT FOUL. WHO WAS THE FOUL ON?

60
58
8
SMITH
webull

Alanna Smith! A Lynx foul meant two free throws for the Liberty. Lynx coach Cheryl Reeve challenged the call, but it was unsuccessful. Stewart took the free throws and made them both. Now the score was tied. The game went into overtime, and the Liberty had all the **momentum**.

With 10.1 seconds left in overtime, Stewart was on the free throw line again. She landed two more free throws. In a history-making moment, the Liberty won 67–62. It was the first championship in the **franchise's** history. It was also the first overtime championship in WNBA history.

TIME OUT

In the final game, the Liberty had 25 free throws to the Lynx's eight.

Was the Liberty victory a clean win? Not everyone thought so, and many blamed the officials' foul call on Smith. The contact between players was brief and a natural part of basketball. When the late-game foul call and free throws sent the game into overtime, everything changed.

Did the officials make the right call? Or did they change the outcome of the game—and history—with the call?

You have replaced one of the officials on the court.

There are 5.2 seconds left in the game. Breanna Stewart catches the inbounds pass.

She aims for the hoop, briefly knocking into Alanna Smith as she shoots.

Was there a contact foul?

If so, Coach Reeve of the Lynx challenges your call and wants a review.

CHAPTER 3

OFFICIALLY AN ERROR

It was a heated battle between the New York Knicks and the Houston Rockets on February 12, 2024. The clock was winding down, and the score was tied at 103. Only seconds remained as Knicks forward Precious Achiuwa **blocked** a shot by Rockets guard Jalen Green.

Aaron Holiday, another Rockets guard, picked up the loose ball. He tried for a long shot. Knicks guard Jalen Brunson jumped to block the ball. As the ball bounced off the rim, the buzzer sounded. But the game wasn't over.

OFFICIALS CALLED A FOUL, BUT ON WHOM?

The foul was on Brunson! Time left on the clock: 0.3 seconds. Brunson was shocked! He had tried to block the ball, but he hadn't touched it. Plus he went right back into position after.

There was contact between Brunson and Holiday, but that was after the ball was released. Brunson pleaded his case to the official, but it didn't matter.

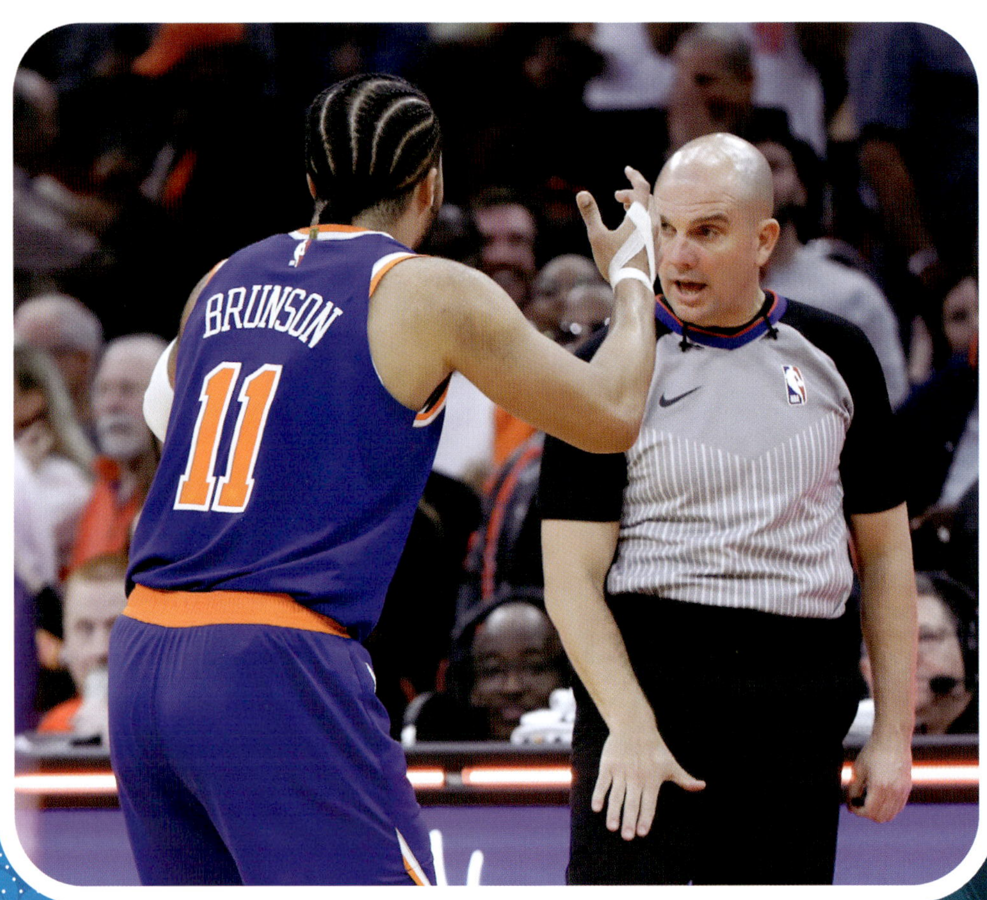

The officials watched the replay and gave Holiday three free throws. Holiday made the first two, giving the Knicks the lead. Taking his last shot, he missed on purpose. He just wanted to run out the last 0.3 seconds of play and keep the score at 105–103. It was a fair **tactic**, and it worked. The Rockets won the game!

The next day, the head referee spoke to the media. He said that after another replay review when the game was over, the foul call on Brunson was a mistake. But it didn't change the outcome of the game.

TIME OUT

The Knicks protested the incorrect foul call with the NBA. But the NBA ruled that errors made by officials were not a reason to bring the teams together to replay the end of the game.

It's your first game as an NBA official, and there are 0.3 seconds left.

Rockets guard Aaron Holiday leaps in the air to attempt a long shot.

Knicks guard Jalen Brunson jumps up to block the shot. While in the air, the players briefly collide.

Was there a contact foul?

If so, Knicks Coach Tom Thibodeau wants a review.

CHAPTER 4

REPLAY REVERSAL

On May 31, 2018, the stakes were high in Game 1 of the NBA Finals. There were 36 seconds left in the game. The Cleveland Cavaliers had a two-point lead. Then, Golden State Warriors forward Kevin Durant drove to the basket. Cavaliers forward LeBron James moved in to block him.

The players made contact. Officials called a charging foul on Durant. This would give the Cavaliers the ball. But before moving on, the officials decided to review the video.

WHEN THEY SAW THE REPLAY, WHAT DID THEY DECIDE?

THEY CHANGED THEIR MINDS!

They reversed the call and **charged** James with a blocking foul instead. Officials gave Durant two free throws, which he landed to create a 104–104 tie. The game went into overtime! And the reversed foul call, free throw points, and extra play gave the Warriors a **morale** boost.

The Warriors Klay Thompson sank a three-pointer. Shaun Livingston hit a mid-range jumper. The Warriors won the game 124–114. But the questions continued.

No one could deny Durant and James made contact. Some said officials had to call a foul on one of them. Others thought it was too late in the game. Some said the replay review never should have happened. They said officials didn't have questions about where the contact happened on the court. That meant the replay wasn't legal according to the rules.

You are an official, closely watching the last 36 seconds of the game.

Golden State Warriors forward Kevin Durant drives to the basket for a shot.

Cavaliers forward LeBron James comes close to block. The players make contact.

Was there a foul?

If so, which player was at fault?

As you can tell, the job of a basketball official isn't easy. Most of the time, they get the calls right. But they might change their minds about a call. And anytime a call is controversial, fans, players, and coaches are going to be upset. The next time you're watching basketball, pay extra attention to the officials. They have a high-stakes role in this fast-paced game.

Do you have what it takes to be a referee someday?

COULD YOU MAKE THE CALL?

GLOSSARY

block (BLOK)—to stop a ball from going into the hoop

charge (CHARJ)—being held accountable for something

conclusion (kuhn-KLOO-shuhn)—a decision based on facts available

destined (DES-tind)—certain or meant to be

franchise (FRAN-chize)—a sports organization

momentum (moh-MEN-tuhm)—strength gained by a series of events

morale (muh-RAL)—the feelings or state of mind of a person or group of people

precise (pri-SAHYS)—very accurate or exact

tactic (TAK-tik)—a planned method

upheld (uhp-HELD)—given support

READ MORE

Berglund, Bruce. *Basketball GOATs: The Greatest Athletes of All Time*. North Mankato, MN: Capstone Press, 2021.

Chandler, Matt. *Basketball's Origin Story*. North Mankato, MN: Capstone Press, 2025.

Kjartansson, Kjartan Atli. *Stars of the NBA: Second Edition*. New York: Abbeville Kids, 2024.

INTERNET SITES

National Basketball Hall of Famers
hoophall.com/hall-of-famers

Say Yes to Officiating
sayyestoofficiating.com/become-a-sports-official/sports/basketball

Sports Illustrated Kids: Basketball
SIKids.com/basketball

INDEX

ABOUT THE AUTHOR

Heather E. Schwartz writes children's books on a wide variety of topics. She lives in upstate New York with her husband, two kids, and two cats.